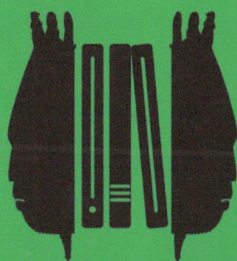

BLACK LEGACY PRESS™

WWW.BLACKLEGACYPRESS.ORG

ANANSI AND THE WITCH

AS RETOLD BY
UWA AFU

ANANSI AND THE WITCH

As Retold By
Uwa Afu

BLP PUBLISHING
Eastchester New York

For wholesale please visit:
www.BBWLogistics.com

Available wherever books are sold.

ISBN: 978-1-63652-123-7

Anansi, the spider, lived in a village where famine and drought were all over the land, and everyone had to figure out a way to survive.

In the same village was a witch named "Five." She hated her name and cast a spell so that if anyone used her name, they would fall asleep for a whole year.

Anansi said, "AHA! I will trick someone into saying her name and I'll have food for my spider family.

He had saved a little bit of corn and made five piles out of it. He sat on one pile and called Mrs. Rabbit, "Hey, Mrs. Rabbit! Would you like some corn for your children?" Of course, Mrs. Rabbit as she came running.

Anansi told her, if you tell me how many piles of corn there are then I'll let you have one of them!"

Mrs. Rabbit counted, "One-Two-Three-Four-Five." When she said the witch's name, she immediately fell asleep.

Anansi took the rabbit home to his wife, who cooked it. They had food for weeks. But as the food was running out, Anansi decided to try his trick again.

This time he chose Mr. Squirrel. Mr. Squirrel counted the piles and he fell asleep just like Mrs. Rabbit. Anansi took the squirrel home and his family had food for several weeks.

Soon the food was running out again. This time he set his sights on Mrs. Goose. Now Mrs. Goose knew Anansi was a not to be trusted and so she was cautious and attentive .Sitting on his pile of corn, Anansi told Mrs. Goose to count the piles and she could have them.

Mrs. Goose smiled and counted, "One-Two-Three-Four.... .. plus, the pile you are sitting on!!" Anansi got angry and said, "NO!NO! That's not the way to count! Do it right!"

Mrs. Goose smiled and counted, "One-Two-Three-Four...and the one you are sitting on!!" Anansi was so angry he jumped up and down shouting, "NO! NO! That's not the way to count!! You were supposed to say one-two-three-four-five!"

As soon as he said the witch's name he fell asleep.

Not only had Mrs. Goose tricked Anansi, she had......how many piles of corn?